THE AMERICANS

PITT POETRY SERIES

Ed Ochester, Editor

FOR RACHEL

Nous sommes tous Américains.

Jacques Chirac

CONTENTS

☆

Dear Suburb,   3

After de Tocqueville   5

On the Bullet Train from Hiroshima   7

Letter to Shara in Amman   8

Build Your Dream Home Here   10

California Clouds   11

Dear Suburb,   13

Target   14

Love Field   16

Ambassador Hotel   19

Terra Incognita   21

Pale Tornado   23

Dear Suburb,   25

Self-Portrait as David Lynch   27

In My Name   29

Koi   32

Self-Portrait as David Hockney   33

Western Wind   34

☆

Pastoral   37

Akhmatova's Ashtray   38

44 Standish Avenue   40

35 Miller Drive   42

Green Fields   44

13 Pleasant Street   49

New Directive   50

Landscape with Tyrian Purple   52

Dear Suburb,   54
Thoreau's Beans   55
As When Drought Imagines Fire   57
Passionflower   58
Dear Suburb,   63
The Locusts   65
Running Brush   66
Dear Suburb,   67
Eros and Dust   68
Running Brush   69
Faithful See Virgin Mary in Office Window   70

☆

Notes   75
Acknowledgments   77

Dear Suburb,

I'm not interested in sadness,
just a yard as elder earth,
a library of sunflowers
battered by the night's rain.
When sliced wide, halved at dawn,
I see how you exist,
O satellite town, your bright possibility
born again in drywall
and the diary with the trick lock.
For years I slept with
my window cracked open,
wanting screen-cut threads of rain.
Blind suburb, dear untruth,
you who already know what I mean
when I praise every spared copse,
you were my battery, my sad clue,
but after I mowed the lawn
and watched robins chesting
for seeds, I couldn't resist
what hung in the toolshed
where, with a pair of garden shears,
I cut all the hair from my arms. That need,
that scared need to whiten
or clean a surface: plywood or lawn,
and the spywall behind which I stood,
stock-still, and sinned against
the fly's flyness. Though you live
inside me, though you laid eggs
in the moisture at the corners
of my eyes, I still dream about
your sinking empire twenty feet above

sea level, and the many things
you fail to see: beautiful bleached
gas can, tomato posts bent into art,
how half of a butterfly, cut crosswise,
still looks like a butterfly, etc.

After de Tocqueville

Rather the ice than their way, said Eric the Red.
Or think of Cortez, who burned his ships
on a Mexican beach so his men couldn't

mutiny and cruise home. We're happiest
when drinking and dancing and giving
our daughters away. Our people waited

on landings to board packet ships and steamers.
They clapped to a fiddle or handmade
drum wherever the sea tang was bracing,

then sailed not for cities of gold
or to scan panoramas but to bugger up
drinks and dance. This land is our land

and your land and such. If you go back
and read the accounts, there are many
entries about the wind. Must nostalgia

walk like a prince through all our rooms?
Every Coyote leading a pack over
the border knows it's not the tale that pleases,

it's the telling. Satchmo backstage, mopping
his brow, said, *In every city I've gotta hear lions roar.*
There's this sense we've ravished every petal

from Columbus's flower. Maybe we're better
off when our heroes are personal, when they
fade in the fumes of the Moose Lodge

or die in a shoebox of Polaroids on a closet floor.
We're happiest when drinking and dancing,
next happiest in leisure, then work, then prayer.

In every anthem we hum at the stadium,
caps at our sides, we ignore crops wasted,
vacant stores. Why do we love the apocryphal—

a cherry tree falling—but forget the Choctaw
sending money to feed the starving Irish
just sixteen years after the Trail of Tears?

Wherever we came from, we left mules
and gulls behind. But somehow we swept
rain into our disposition. We feel clouds

gathering—miles above the sugar-beet
region and agro-farms based in Topeka.
Did they ever exist, de Soto's green fountain

or the threshed abundance on Cather's floor?
Newer, faster. Behind our heat is a fever.
Even in religious fervor, said our prince

Walt Whitman, there's a touch of animal heat.
Maybe only a truly great stranger can see it.
Said Kerouac to Robert Frank, *You got eyes.*

On the Bullet Train from Hiroshima

A hundred-fifty through the paddied fields.
It's not the speed that unnerves me,
it's this feeling I get when I look through

tempered glass. Fishermen hunched on buckets.
Forests of trees with their skins peeled back.
It's hard to believe we've tweaked the physics,

pared friction from sleek machines—
like this porpoise-nosed engine hushing the rush.
Even my seat on the aisle seems pleased

with its shape. It's my privilege, I guess,
to relax, if I can shake the calm memorial:
children in the galleries, on the walls

pictures framing the smoke and wrack.
Chains of paper swans. Melted cameras.
A kimono's pattern burned into a woman's back.

Letter to Shara in Amman

A tree of despair grows inside me, strengthens,
on days like today when I'm the worst
kind of lazybones and Olivia naps in my lap.
Outside, birds chip the air. I should be
raking leaves. While pushing the stroller
this morning I felt the welling of materials
around me—airbrushed cars, a half-caned chair
by the curb—and paused when I saw a blue jay
flattened on the street. I wondered how
you'd write about its colors splayed
faux-angelic, its runty raptored bones.
I've always envied how you chance upon
a scene and make a tiny biography of its things.
Soon you'll lie near a desert shore and with your
new son look a long way up into the sky.
Where's your city? Do the mosques admit you?
When I was young I saw everything
through a lens of faith. I can't explain what
I was looking for beyond the animals—
God maybe. It had something to do with
my divided self. Crazy Hart Crane had it right:
My only final friends—the wren and thrush,
made solid print for me across dawn's broken arc.
That communion, that awe—I crave it,
but all I can do is watch football and stroke
Olivia's hair. Last fall, a few moments
after she was born, I cut the cord.
The scissors shook in my fingers. I didn't
feel the surpassing power I'd expected.
Flowers arrived from nowhere. She slept.
I miss California where we drank good coffee

and always talked about grace. Now I stroll
over the painted moisture of the leaves.
There are too many days when we can't be
done with anything, when we *dwell*,
but soon our children will grow and point
to things, and remind us that a rabbit's child is
a bun, and a bird's child is a chick, and a worm's
child is two worms, and a sky can have as its child
a forest, and a river can have as its child a sea.

Build Your Dream Home Here

        First the towers
fell, then the Dow. A few years later,
while she was still recovering
from the blind fumbling accounts
of people crushed to dust—
her nights chocked with emergencies,
smoke, the newsfeed, the taped
and sniffed envelopes, the falling—
that's when they'd built the place,
a roomy number bricked back
from the corner. A bank offered
low interest, veterans no down.
In every closet they'd make love.
They'd space out the bushes, lay toast
and coffee on the porch.
        It worked
for a while, their screened-in story,
where a half-deflated soccer ball
wedged the door. Drunk on lilac,
they cheered whenever a bee seemed
to veer off course.
        Now boxes packed
with their belongings cover the lawn.
She checks the buttons on her blouse
and worries about her husband's
smoking. Will the lilacs survive?
Will their mild, wilting odor still lure
the bees? In some parts of the world,
the wood of the lilac is carved
into knife handles or flutes. *Līlek*,
from the Arabic, meaning "slightly blue."

California Clouds

You were never young; you knew it
        each morning when the light pulled
its gauze from some carefully selected

        part of your body—ankle, chin—
and you felt, in view of that great reaching
        mist dissolving inland, like a blow-up

doll bitten too hard by its lover.
        Then you staggered through fog
to follow the rules of the coffee house

        (only an hour in the socket), saw kids
on bikes accompanied on Bernal Hill,
        until the gab inside Progressive Grounds

whipped your eyes alive. The crow-haired
        barista with the cherub tattoo was
saying up there, by the tower, is where

        the coyote lives. She'd seen it.
All the cats on alert. You still want
        to know how it happened, howling

above so much domestic life, *inside* it:
        gravel and tasted bait. O grovel.
O flatbed lovers and kids climbing

        hand over fist—they pencil in the slated
sky and kink the chains of time.
        You never shunned safety. When you

tried it for the first time, saké tasted
    like oblivion. (Let's move to the third
person point of view, as it's clearer.)

    He returned, deleted, returned. Bills
racked up. Women thought he was something
    of a limp-fish. He never finished

his masterpiece titled "Self-Portrait
    as a Crucible of Style." Mirrors he hated
and weeks of slinking, and when he hiked

    the hill and found the coyote with two
holes in its side, he cried for its howling,
    that creature, his low cortege of clouds.

Dear Suburb,

Some blunt hammering set me off,
that and the teeth of a saw.
I left behind my sweater,
the remains of a sandwich, my camera,
some paperweights, my lament. I left behind
a few weak coals I'd blown alive.
This happened somewhere
off one of your forgotten roads,
just past a farm stand where customers leave
a little corrugated shed
with the smell of rotting corn silk in their clothes.
The important *f*s are *focus*, *flatness*, and *frame*.
If your billboards peel, if the gaze
is really dead, then what are those remaining
fields to you—are they the clothing
of thought, or the mirror of thought,
or just thought's sleeping sheets?

Target

In this land
of no origin
we wheeled plastic carts

and carried on
in the cardboard trade

as if we'd lost
somehow
our tribal sense of space.

The sun grew
into the center
of the day
and baked the parking lot's text.

We failed to see
the sun's face
was aimed,

how it burned
through an ancient mane.

Gold cooled in its eyes.
Its tail twitched,
lackadaisical,

while we sped
through filtered air.

Did we know
we were the last
of the shorn beasts?

Yes.

But dazed in traffic,
our streets' by-and-by,

we failed to hear
that lion above saying,

You there, in the dark, you.
Job shaved his head,
but still the lice bit him.

Love Field
November 22, 1963

First, a black mark in the sky,
        a speck that grows

into a plane widening,
            dramatically circling
before it touches
        a gray strip of land
designed for its landing.

Then the players descend
        the wheeled stair

to the stage
        for the cameras,
our collective eye:

        first her, then him,
as is custom,
        and their entourage
trailing behind,

        those who believe
the world is young
        and the future spreads
out like geography.

It's the beginning
        of all that,
        and what a show it is,

the bouquet of roses
       we see given to her
on the scratchy screen,

the film pouring its light,
       edges burned.

And who knows what's truth,
       what's myth,
or if they arrive
       as hawks or doves,

brave with risk
       in a bright and swirling
land where the dust
seems to crown
       from its own gray dust.

Here's the raw footage.
       Here's the film
clicking in the projector,

and, as all things seen
       through it
       are black and white,
isn't it important to note

       her roses are red
and not yellow,

and that neither of them
squints in the bright Texas sun?

If you can stand
          what the light inside
the darkness does
          to your eyes,
          watch them pause there
for a moment:
          our champion, our grace,

in that high noon
          that holds all
the freshness of the morning.

Ambassador Hotel
June 5, 1968

You have to read the reports
and ricochets and blunt trauma

in the walls of the greasy kitchen
down the hallway's throat, then return

to your own hearing and back up
a few frames, rewind. You have to rattle

in the drum of the revelry leading to
the shots, yes, and scroll

to see the faces when he says
. . . and now it's on to Chicago, and let's win there.

You have to hope the man
at the podium is building a storm

we'll want to enter, that its gale winds
will feed our rescuing power.

There are men who set charges
that will buckle a structure's beams

and iron struts. Maybe the storm
is inevitable, like the drawn-out struggle

for the gun. When he was young
the candidate hated being touched,

but if you hunch over pictures,
he's reaching for the people of Watts.

There's an old Irish proverb that goes,
Surround yourself with rising water

and the flood will teach you to swim.
As the crowd lifts him down the hallway,

caught in one long, blurred shot,
all we can see from here is

his trailing wake. The hotel collapsed,
is still collapsing. *Is there a doctor in the house?*

We need someone now to save the body
politic, and a rag to mop up the blood.

Terra Incognita

Counting scars of gum on the stairs down
from the Dome I briefly felt joy

even though I'd just read, in the *World* or *Times*,
that some of my fellow citizens

led men to warehouses or sites lost
in chalk republics, where they asked questions

in English and then, when they couldn't grasp
the answers, zapped skin, brain, and bones

to kingdom come. While I drank like a lush
it happened. While I washed down

a pastry with a divine swipe of cheese inside.
My hunger deepened in rundown

churches and cabs. Spooning soup and eyeing
the news, I thought being an American

isn't like being from one of the old nations—
it's not a gift exactly, but it's also

not something to take lightly or give away.
I pictured dawn drawing over it,

the sun hammering its domes. The campaigns
were ramping up, yet here I was eating

fries in a piazza, watching boys loop string
around a pigeon's neck. Mostly I got

what I wanted, forgot what I was,
until a driver in dark shades turned to me

and said, "Your people, whoever they are,
aren't ready for a woman president,

let alone a black." I said nothing, then flogged
myself for days until, stomping up Vesuvius,

I sucked deep the fog that still smelled like ash.
Then I walked down again, thinking about all

those faces in the city below—what a shocking fate
for a single blast's gas to settle on

that populace, to crumple like paper all its lungs.

Pale Tornado

You skirted us again, our homes,
our dead who no longer feel saliva
in their mouths. Some of them
were lucky, that is, short-lived,
since the whirlwind that your angels
offered grew into a golden door.
I want to say we were in
mourning when we welcomed you,
born as you were from a great
glowing mass on a screen
where a man, staring at his Doppler,
murmured out of earshot
not once in thirty-three years . . .
He gazed at his screen
while you rose from our own loose dust.
What is my sight craving
always but cinema, each eye
a theater with the volume dialed
down? Tell me if our dust
feels guilty for lending you skin.
I'm trying to remember what
our weatherman said:
It's very important at a time like this . . .
then later reporting in front
of crushed, shining silos—
At the time it didn't look that impressive.
I saw your halo as something
we shared before winds
dropped and surrounded us:
termite mounds taller than grass,

our fencerows and homes up for auction.
If we're lucky, we're short-lived—
and when you touched down, breathing heavy,
I was standing next to some guy,
I think it was Gary Dobbs, who said,
"My God, look at that thing—it's huge."

Dear Suburb,

Must you tremble
when cars trap shadows,

or when the neighbor's apricots,
terribly bitter,

fall on the lawn at night?
Like the vine and trellis,

I want to hug you from behind
the way a friend

surprises a friend.
Awake beneath my bedspread,

the stars' crooked branches,
I also need the calm

of a child's boxed beach.
We've carved our feathers

to the smallest shavings.
Our hairs grow gray.

Something yet lives wild
in our nettled dens.

The dead return
as lampposts, gas guzzlers,

gnats frenzied
in a laptop's moonish glow.

Said another way:
there's something fraught

about this night
that knows our whereabouts,

its weight pressing down on us,
Wake up, wake up.

Self-Portrait as David Lynch

I wear a flower in my lapel.
I like the sweetness of its lie in my nose.
A carnation, the fool's flower,

its heart a wilting empire.
In late-night editing sessions,
I imagine I'm planting flowers

in the sockets of eyes. Whatever helps
me reach our rigor mortis,
bound behind the wheel,

a little Bowie on the radio, maybe,
at six frames per second,
headlights plowing the dark's divided road.

Cities grow to calcified castles.
Fish groom the coral brains
anchored in a tank's purple volume.

I love the scratch of celluloid
and a low-register noise,
the hair of heat burning in a lit bulb.

Sometimes I swap my carnation
for an orchid or rose.
On-screen, there's every hint

a man-child built the night.
I read it once, by flashlight, as a kid—
that Sleep and Death are brothers,

and they send our dreams through two gates,
one made of horn, for the true dreams,
and one made of tusk, for the false.

In My Name

Like the *Necessary Evil* and *Enola Gay*,
in a sphere of air that's calm and mildly cool,
I need some last grip of blue to trigger
my sleep. It was technically flawless,
that mission, as they'd dropped a few
dry-run pumpkins with a bird's-eye scope.
When I close my eyes under the drone of a fan,
I see planes rattling in the aftermath.
Smoothly soldered rivets saved the men inside.
At a commemoration the captain said,
"I'm proud I started with nothing
and made it work as perfectly as it did."
Then, when the press persisted, red flashing
his face: "Hey, I sleep clear every night."

I lie in another state, placeless in the air,
with the sound of occasional sirens
or barking dogs. In a magazine
I read about *Predators* over Pakistan,
our drone with fifty eyes named *Gorgon Stare*.
The men at Langley, bombing by remote,
call a person who escapes their fire, who runs
from a car or burning hut, a *squirter.*
Night is sometimes an acid, sometimes a cure.
In other words, *homo fabula*: we're part human,
part story, but our mouths pass on in silence.
I think of the men who brought that silence:
Mr. Harry S. Truman, Captain Paul Tibbets,
who painted his mother's name on the nose
of the plane.
                    My dream house circles me.

Peonies thrive in beds I forget to water.
With pillows I lie. A white cotton sheet covers
my chest. I've been told to sleep in peace,
where the trees are crowned with plenty
and where birds float through wood-lawn,
broom, and shrubs. Where a found twig
can be golden or mundane. To orchestrate
my sleep I take a pill, and as I fade finally,
at the time of night when the birds believe
they're leaves, I dream of a path in acacia
season where the air smells lemony
and my whole day seems to rest on the limbs
of the trees. Suddenly, a siren sound.
Wind ripping the valley after a flash . . .

In Plymouth, spring of '45, while the Pacific
squadrons trained, my father was born
without cataracts in his eyes—*David Roderick*,
7 lbs., asleep on his mother's white gown.
There must have been milk and a huge cloud
of necessity in which they breathed.
In August, before he could talk, neutrons
sheared from a core. I've read what they left behind:
shrines' ashes, and the boy under his desk
who sang all day while his classmates
fell silent, one by one. Two concussions hit
the planes. They roared away from the light
they'd made, the rain.
                                        At night, when I falter
again, and the pill dissolves in my veins,
I think of Langley's coffee, its infrared eyes.

I think of the *Enola Gay* parked in the Smithsonian,
where a woman smashed a jar of blood on its wing.
When I signed my mortgage, I also signed
for the peonies and for the shield of my yard's
tall trees. The birds daub nests of twigs
and human hair. My potting shed makes its
own black sense of heat. Here's the price I pay
for sleeping: *Reapers* circling a far-off village,
my drones. To eyes at a distance, a screen
lies always between a failure and a dream.
In other words, *homo fabula*: we're part story,
part human, but only if our names are known,
and only if our names, when spoken aloud,
are pronounced correctly, with proper inflection,
as when a mother addresses her son.

Koi

Gray or calico, black again, golden-rouge,

they turn and glide. They churn.

Untranslatable,

they feed in my shadows. Above

a heron judges; my face

warped to a Noh mask—white, washed out.

Self-Portrait as David Hockney

I craved a place away from the cold,
where I could Coke bottle

and muscle-tee and see as Eve's snake
must have seen: chromatically,

a torn creation collaged by lovers outdoors.
I wanted treasure unburied,

a hint of gold that would finally lead me astray.
Cheap acrylics. A line's longing

on the canvas of a body.
On my patio I fell in love with voices

cured by cigarettes and lemon fizz.
Where there are no insects, there are no birds.

In California I never chased after a color.
I slept on towels that absorbed

what I'd tasted: chlorine painted on skin.
There, in the vent of my swimming,

afternoons froze the palms,
and I used quick local movements

to pull ripples behind me, and under
the blush of a swimming pool,

I unslippered from my hole
toward warmth that never speaks or goes away.

Western Wind

Enough, wind, enough. You tire me
with the miles you've covered, with your face
whiskering my sill. I'm trying to sleep.
You've hauled me enough, you've run
before me luffing and coursing about. Disking,
kiting up, stroking my front hedge.
I'm hard alee and creaking inside you. In irons.
Under clouds. Stop leading me
to believe the box that birthed
you was beautiful. At night I breathe
the lark's dark. In the hangar air
of an office building, I swear
I'd be happier without you. When I drag
bins to the curb or jog this whole
neighborhood on a leash,
you're always raising the hair on my arms
and making the older trees bend over me—
those great afflicted trees. You think
I don't have desires like Coleridge in his bower
or Vincent Millay stewing in
her claw-foot tub? I want to believe
in your paws, your raining sleeves. But I'm not
just some grass you've touched.
I'm a baritone who might have been happy
had I learned how to sing.

Pastoral

Birds graze the tassels,
        sparrowing actually, or mocking,
their colors worth
        nothing unless I pin
        their wings
            in the field.
Speaking of fields:
        the Russians say
        life is a walk across an open one
where mules are buried,
        and men.
        The soil remembers
a forest that marched right through.
In time-lapse.
        In the filtered light
        a camera peels from wheat.
I see soldiers' hands, too,
        grazing the tassels.
If you think you're here
        with me, feeling the field
on you, chained to it
        like a peasant,
        aging like good wine and cheese,
            you are.
Having noticed the sparrows,
        you notice the flies.
Having heard a bell,
        you see some cows,
        together on an upland slope.

Akhmatova's Ashtray

Wolves climb her stairs
    to sniff along
    the back of her wardrobe,
paw her clothes,
        but all they smell is smoke.

Someone wrote
a requiem and never claimed it.
      Someone bombed
all the shops.

      It happened
in Leningrad:
plaster flaking,
        her small concert
   of words
sung through a gate.

    The little engine of history
    plows through snow.

Someone blacked
    the domes to foil the bombers.
         Stay, endure.
    Someone cut
her clothesline, stole her shoes.

      In the queue
along the prison wall,
    waiting for news
    of her son,

she memorizes
bricks
and wishes for
　　　a basket with sun clothed
over it,
　　　　　beneath the wool
　　　　　　　some bread
　　　　　　　or a green pear.

In her head
a rhythm holds
　　　the words, so when she hears
claws on her stairs,
　　　　　　a gust
on the hall's parquet,

　　　　she lights
　　　　with her cigarette
　　a white scrap,
　　　　　　grinds it to ash.

To you, our loneliness together,
　　　　　　I raise my glass.

Can't I make something
      of her bed, our sleep,
and the white seam
opening between us,
      our shared afternoons
in the rendition house
      where my nursing ended
and trying-to-be-perfect
began, when I was swept
      into forbiddance,
then tucked down,
her body my lean-to
      after an hour of knitting
(in which her voice
vibrated accordingly),
      not long before
I borrowed her Irish sigh?
She was the spine
      and I was the cross
and both of us knew
the curse of a blind
      mole burrowing.
When we lay with each other
      in her bed,
the point was to be still,
not to sleep, but she fell
      anyway while animals
passed over us, plastic stars.
      Above I saw a spider's
testimony, and pink walls,

until in my first dream,
          a crow landed on my chest
and pecked at my face,
meaning, as I now believe,
          that I should have listened
when she said *this is how*
you burrow, this is how
          you knead, this is how you
hold your breath in a tunnel.

35 Miller Drive

My mother knew it was a fault to love
a place, to believe a cure

for hunger lived in the ground.
In July shade, that dark torch

burning in the air between us,
she watered dirt, broke beans,

clipped leaves with her scissors' eye.
She said if we separated

magnet from root, killed
beetles and mealworms, slugs,

we wouldn't fail if the rain came
and spoiled the soil with guilt.

The moon warps vegetables
with incubations and foils,

and to such elements I was
sensitive—the nipple given, half-wet,

the dirt that cries for its milk.
Years later, I still feel its pull

and confess I want to return
to that place, sun on my shoulders

and face, where I might revive
that garden, channel its water,

and tend it like a mother who stays
with her dead child, who won't let go,

who sleeps in the same bed with it.

Green Fields

1. *The Legend of St. Brigid*

She was a poor girl minding her cow
and had no place to feed it but the roadside.

Then a rich man who owned the land
came by and in a fit of pity said,
"How much land would it take to give grass to the cow?"

"As much as my cloak will cover,"
she answered, and the man said, "I will give that."

She laid down her cloak then, and it spread
out miles on every side, wool unfolding
shadows of fields, the hills like warmth rushing in.

But soon a silly old woman came by
and stopped and said, "If your cloak goes on
spreading, our whole island will be free,"

and with that the cloak stopped and spread no more.

2. *Descendancy*

Work: sowing what we could in a bog-seam
        until the lumper failed us, the horse potato,

the patron saint of butter. We couldn't pay.
        Without a handle on our hunger, heather lay

crudely over the land. We did what we could.
        Now we curse the bailiff's turf and around

our cottage bank a fair fire. So what if our
        muscles spindle to thread? Bear witness.

Watch while our nets split from witchery
        and crops bleed frost on a plank of dew.

Your name will be honored as ours are,
        forgotten. The cottage will kneel to scalpeen

and burn the grass around: scorched reeds,
        mustard needled to flame and crested soot.

We're your roots and heat. You're our cuttings
        stashed in a pocket. The air flexes

through old stone, dampened vine and stem.
        The walls un-vetch and chimney flies naked.

If our people can't have it, nobody will—
        this ink surviving, an *X* on onionskin paper.

3. *Groomers*

Tumbling from sky the buzzards
sweep fetchless, legs rearing out
and down as they land. Their knived faces,
voices claw-like: *Hark, what goes here?*
You wouldn't think it,
but each has its own character:
Bald Bitch, The Warden, The Pillar of Pall.
They're studied. You'll never touch
the artifice of their masks
or smell their breath, like rot.
Before approaching, they talk,
settling things. It's a privilege, really,
the company of their flock.
One of them flicks your hair, flaps back,
then they rummage your clothes by the roadside.

4. *Steerage*

The ships they boarded had names:
    Izette, Village Bell.

The sea had another name: *Gleaner.*

    Fields swept
to ocean
      the younger siblings,

blessed by a boot's glorious kick.

Onto the *Magnet* they climbed,
    the *Queen Victoria*;

they kipped on the *General Green.*

Falling into the dance
    of trying to keep balance,

    "Let our legs be
strong and plumb," they prayed,

"Let the jack-in-the-sails
    drown with his jug any flame."

5. *Their Ship Near Its Longing*

Home was an island moored to an empire.

      Home was a blister of blood in the yolk.

Home was the storm that broke the mast

      when nobody warned the colleens.

Home was a biscuit wrapped in a kerchief.

      Home was a kerchief draped on a face.

One way, launched from the harbor at Cobh

      as they keened the magpie's gray.

Home was beyond the valleys of sea,

      a drink for the picker, a drink for the drum.

Home was a prospect, those last few waves

      toward the shuttles of Lowell's looms.

13 Pleasant Street

What not to touch: boiling handkerchiefs,
a leech beneath a flagstone, writhing.

She scrubbed blood with ammonia,
poured bleach on coffee or grass,

fuller's earth for oil or a splash of wine.
Those were the days with pins in her mouth.

In mine: *C is for collar. D is for dress.*
Only our forks and spoons were stainless.

She never let the wrong substance set.
And where the birds sang over us

their instructions, I stood with her
while she pinned all our clothes in the wind,

whatever we'd slept in, whatever shrank
before the end of its season,

our cottons, our towels and sheets—
the way they moved, the way they moved.

New Directive

"First there's the children's
house of make believe . . . "

Here's what happens
when you flee the switch's flick.
Flies follow you.
The happiness you were promised
knifes the night.
Children know—
they know a touch
of squill here, a little wild onion
there. They know Judas
Iscariot hanged
himself from an aspen,
its bark scarred with mold
and oystered scales.
Imagine: a disciple splashing
his rust on a whitewashed trunk.
Crowds scare the children.
Their houses say *odor,*
say *whiskered sleep.*
Someone snores through
the wall where
their beds are bridged.
They dream about siblings
who stir up hives
or return from the pond
with a moon-streak,
permanent, in their hair.
Look for them.
You'll never find their dishes,
their goblet or knives.

You gape at screens.
You're dreaming up places
where the real news is made.
Forgiveness for you,
if it exists, is a nail hammered in tar.
Or it's the little white flower
you never, to this day,
learned the name of.

Landscape with Tyrian Purple
Morocco

Children pry snails from the rocks
as if hunting for Tyrian purple,
that dye that had fetched its weight

in silver and, when prized by the Romans,
gold. We'd traveled far by then,

through Arabic and French, hoping
to see the famous color, its fever
"like the pulse of a Berber horse

trained for war." I read all the conquerors
cut through those northern hills.

For two euros and a lipstick the shade
of an animal's wound, a woman
painted henna on my wife's hands.

Our guide said Essaouira was "fond
for holidays": Jet Skis and camel rides,

golf played along "beaches of rose and blood."
The children worked best, since their hands
fit the rocks—surfaces gulled

by time, pocked and cemented,
picked over. At the height of empire

barrels of snails were left to spoil
in the medina. Ten thousand shells
dyed a single sash. First emperors killed

for it, then popes. I could stand
in place and say nothing or double

the length of my shadow at dusk or dawn.
What I can't do is say I saw the color,
like a queen's ocean, where camels

ambled out to the spit's end. My mood
relates often to a view of the hills,

and now my fondest memory of that place
is the long ride to the airport where,
on the rocky, barren land

I saw a shepherd, in a gown and bare feet,
herding, with a forked stick, his tiny flock.

Dear Suburb,

Just once I'd like to come home
to find that you've scattered the pieces
of a saxophone all over my bed.

Thoreau's Beans

Here's where he exists,
his hunger grasping how to cultivate,
then gorge, and now he wakes

inside the dead-mule smell
of lilac around his cottage,
and now he wrestles with roots

in the sun, struggling,
as a husband, with the harness,
and while lancing blisters

he remembers the view
from Ktaadn, how a cloud
soaked him on its upper slope—

no brother but the self—
and he returns meek among
the asphodel even more determined

that his crop will thrive,
becoming almost desperate
for long pails of water,

while beneath him is what
he summons: brute feet,
his hands smelling like leeks—

in a notebook this is his *thrift*
and *estate*: the stems
weakened until he finds them

cow chips, which he must
have felt for in the dark
but never wrote about stealing

from his neighbors' fields,
and now he sees himself,
without the pond's reflection,

for what he is, a failed guide,
since what's fleeting can't be
guarded: colors of badgers,

the sober points of wrens,
so few words, outlined,
whipped from their oily wings.

As When Drought Imagines Fire

Loot my point of view,
                              hove my heart
              free from its hived booth
though I know your smoke,
                              its black blossom,
is a substance I'll never become:
                    colors
          of plaster and grass I've prepped
flawlessly, rivers I've whittled thin.

It's a personal matter to me, the wind.
But let it be our cathedral feeling:
                              a sculpture
of ash
                    dragging its robe over
the hills because of us,
                              because of me.
Yellow is hurried,
                    but red moves like a swarm
          through toothpick homes,
          pans over roofs,
                    where the ethos we child
                              from the ground
will blacken to ruin.
                              Let's glory
          this roughened nap
of landscape,
                    this parched Arcadia,
with one nude-struck match and a breeze.

Passionflower

1.

First vision: stamens,
        gold sometimes, more often blue,

and the bloom
        that will become a parable

if a large-bodied bee
        pollinates it,

or a hermit bat, or a sword-billed
        hummingbird.

Propagate, wings,
        and be blessed.

2.

While monkeys howled
around them, and a full view
of the mountains watched
them from behind,
they peered through creepers
until a single flower
called, on fire above.
High on its perfume,
they believed it was the flower
in St. Francis's vision,
with a vine that climbed
the cross and fixed
itself where nails
had been driven through
wood, and with their ships
anchored in the harbor,
and guns unbirding
the sky, they named it
Flower of the Five Wounds.

3.

Pizarro's horse ate
the flower without considering
what it meant,

and it's thought
Pizarro himself crushed

its petals and made
perfume for his lover's hair,
and when the scent betrayed him

he had no choice
but to treat his sleeplessness

by drinking its pulp:
flash of armada,
light from the fireflies' range.

4.

Beauty is *in* the eye: spit-pit,
        Judas-hole, which is also the spot

where the fronds grow, covered
        by hairs that exude a sticky mud,

the *wild maracuja* with bugs
        digested inside, the *white poka*

on half-bred pathways,
        stamped by pig hooves, gorged.

5.

Thank God it wasn't the maculate iris,
and not the rose, emblem of secrets
carved into palace walls.

They feasted on the fruit
while the natives, wearing suns
made of gold on their chests,
watched them from the path below.

Then, satisfied with the gift
and agreeing it was a heavenly sign,
the missionaries threw
themselves with great zeal
into converting the natives.

They succeeded in a very short time.

Dear Suburb,

What happened to the golden rule
among all
      your shining objects—

these daisies and grills, these bikes—
      even the dog turd dropped

on my lawn, hidden by a few measly stalks?

      You've made me afraid
to touch clovers and my wife's hidden

      hooks and, most sadly,
            the woolen hats
on my neighborhood's children,

      which in winter are bright fruit.

The next time you text me, I'll be high
      on magnolia pollen

         and munching chips
near the bluebird house,

amazed I can thrive here so close

      to a city's lost eminence,
where you bring a golden stillness
         to everything

I touch, where I go whole years

    without suffering
        so much as a splinter.

The Locusts

Terror from the air.
        Green churning to dread
                three inches deep. From a distance
they take the bittersweet, the rooted

        and twined. All that's left
                to be seen: a building halved,
the icehouse dome. But the farmer,
        his wife and child, they gather

        what they can before the cold
snaps shut. Smallpox hovers
        between them. They never hear
                the cough trapped in their well.

A cloud's honed jaws
        swept their fields, their grass,
                stored corn, bridles and burlap—
everything except a hand-stitched

        doll's buttons-for-eyes.
                Even come winter the child will feel
wings brush past. In broad daylight.
        At night. The road signs, wrong:

        here's where the land was rich,
where birds lacked markings,
        and where a man could sometimes go
                to have a good cry without hiding.

Running Brush

Shoots hug the lake. Beasts hollow. The ice shores out to fallow fur. Once again I wish I could keep from crunching. When Thoreau heard a horn in his depth of woods, with its hardly determined center, it warmed his winter. To him it suggested poise and gave confidence. Maybe it's impossible to draw snow. Through limbs I catch some rosiness, the rim of the sky's black dome. But it's that sound I want, that *sound*. Thoreau wrote it was as friendly as a hermit's candle.

Dear Suburb,

When I say my porch is low
and wide, I mean it's barely a porch, hacking out
roses growing around it, I say there's
enough flush here for a vase,
but you say wait until they're the shade of red
Gauguin dreamed when he painted
children before smearing
their faces, and I say what about
the two men in the rusted van
trolling this neighborhood for kids,
and you say we need shocks
of goldenrod, shocks of crow, and besides
it does no good to pray
for some gleaming day when a bird will
land on you like a catkin, and then
you remind me of the glory
of a city on a hill, which I've tried
in eight different ways to refute,
and you say we both want a hornet at the center
of a screen, and then I confess,
as if you give a damn, that I love
in fact your highways and lawns, these raw
lots developers bought for a song.

Eros and Dust

Sun touches the tin
of hand cream on her nightstand,
and he feels the soft bones
of their bed, its cartilage
bracing them near the wall.
The bed like a drawbridge
and sleep carrying them across it.
With his arm draped
around her, after she's gone
quiet, he feels like a king growing
old inside his castle.
Rather than being
devoured by some myth,
he's drifting far from the scythes
in his fields, the dust
from his stables—safe within a moat
that can't be crossed.

Running Brush

Basho said to refuse a prayer until its warmth hunches inside like a bird in its hutch. First the fledgling is born, then the worm, then they meet somewhere in the grass. I choose my paper for its cereal color, fuss over shaving a pencil. The prayer means to cleanse both triumph and lust. O derivative, sunlight reaping the trees, this whole morning cries through a single reed. Pencil, razor blade, spit—I'll try not to hurry.

Faithful See Virgin Mary in Office Window

In flowerbeds we crowd, some praying,
some bowing as the world, minute as it is,
stays in motion: box stores doing business,

fast-food joints, and above us a crow,
secular bird, lighting on a lamppost
while we take pictures or cry as if we could

live forever in this gloried surround,
gazing up at the window holding her bleared
hair, her mouth a frenzy of trapped

pollen or dust, eyes like smooth shells
that make us forget what fertilized
the flowers at our feet, bulbs fortified

with potash or bone meal, dried blood,
which reminds me of the *Annunziata*
I saw in Italy, painted by those who thought

color itself was divine: crushed shell,
coral and ash, pigments mixed with egg
in a man's mouth, and I worry about

standing too close to the believers, I who
rubberneck and lie, do I stand too close
to the woman at least six months along

with her own child, waving a sonogram
with a faint infant shape inside, the image
scratched by waves: light squandered here,

dilated there, compressed oil and dust
as every body contains its atlas of salt,
kiss-worn, and always some bud dreamed

in springtime, and though I'm a yarner
and one for whom doubt is a clutched root,
I can't yet walk to my car, standing here

wondering if after His birth the virgin girl
saw the rest of her life would be nothing
but a way to talk about that morning:

gold nearly blinding, herdsmen and kings,
and with its broad warm tongue
a cow licking the afterbirth from the hay.

NOTES

"After de Tocqueville": The opening quotation and a few details were borrowed from William Carlos Williams's *In the American Grain*. Robert Frank: "When people look at my pictures, I want them to feel the way they do when they want to read the line of a poem twice." The poem is dedicated to Charlie Bassett.

"Letter to Shara in Amman": The italicized passage is from Hart Crane's poem "A Postscript," as it appears in *Complete Poems of Hart Crane* (Liveright, 2001).

"Self-Portrait as David Lynch" is for Mark Warburton.

"In My Name": "The Predator War," by Jane Mayer (*New Yorker*, October 26, 2009), inspired this piece. Other source material came from *The Bombing of Hiroshima* by Gordon Thomas and Max Morgan Witts.

"Akhmatova's Ashtray": The final two lines are from Anna Akhmatova's "The Last Toast," translated by D. M. Thomas, as it appears in *Selected Poems* (Penguin, 2006).

"Green Fields": Irish ballads, especially "The Green Fields of Amerikay," influenced this poetic sequence. "The Legend of St. Brigid" was reconstructed from chapters in Lady Gregory's *Book of Saints and Wonders*. "Descendancy": In order to spite landowners who planned to evict them, nineteenth-century Irish cottiers often burned their own homes.

The "Running Brush" poems gesture toward the Japanese prose-poetry genre *zuihitsu*. Thanks to Kimiko Hahn, whose book *The Narrow Road to the Interior* brought this form to my attention.

ACKNOWLEDGMENTS

Thank you to the editors of publications in which these poems first appeared, sometimes in alternate formats or with different titles:

American Poetry Review: "Self-Portrait as David Hockney," "Self-Portrait as David Lynch"; *Birmingham Poetry Review*: "Landscape with Tyrian Purple"; *Cave Wall*: "Passionflower"; *Copper Nickel*: "The Locusts"; *Four Way Review*: "Dear Suburb," ("Some blunt hammering set me off..."); *Georgia Review*: "After de Tocqueville"; *Inch*: "Dear Suburb," ("Just once I'd like to come home..."); *Indiana Review*: "Akhmatova's Ashtray"; *Memorious*: "As When Drought Imagines Fire," "35 Miller Drive"; *Meridian*: "California Clouds," "New Directive"; *New Orleans Review*: "Love Field"; *Notre Dame Review*: "Eros and Dust"; *Orion*: "Dear Suburb," ("When I say my porch is low and wide..."); *Poetry*: "Dear Suburb," ("I'm not interested in sadness..."), "Faithful See Virgin Mary in Office Window"; *Poetry Daily*: "Pastoral"; *Quarterly West*: "Running Brush" ("Shoots hug the lake..."); *The Rumpus*: "Target," "Terra Incognita"; *Salt Hill*: "13 Pleasant Street," "44 Standish Avenue"; *Shenandoah*: "Green Fields"; *Southern Review*: "Pastoral," "Running Brush" ("Basho said to refuse a prayer..."); *Slate*: "Thoreau's Beans"; *Two Weeks: A Digital Anthology of Contemporary Poetry*: "Dear Suburb," ("Must you tremble...").

I would like to express gratitude to the trustees of the Amy Lowell Trust for supporting my work at a critical stage and to my colleagues in UNCG's MFA Program for their faith and friendship.

Special thanks to the editors of *Shenandoah* for awarding "Green Fields" the 2012 James Boatwright III Prize for Poetry and to Phillis Levin, Vijay Seshadri, and Elizabeth Spires for selecting a group of these poems as the co-winner of the 2012 Campbell Corner Poetry Prize.

For their critical suggestions and moral support, I'm grateful to Geoff Brock, Keith Ekiss, Robin Ekiss, Jeff Hoffman, Tom Kealey, Megan Snyder-

Camp Lehman, Shara Lessley, Alan Shapiro, Ed Skoog, Julia Ridley Smith, Bruce Snider, Tess Taylor, and C. Dale Young.

Thank you to Ed Ochester for his faith in these poems and to the outstanding editorial and production staff at the University of Pittsburgh Press.

Rodericks, Halls, Finnegans, Richardsons, and Jacksons, you're the best.